T0065492

Ron Lewis

John 3:16

God's Quick Word for a Hurried World

John 3:16

God's Quick Word for a Hurried World

Ron Lewis

WESTBOW
PRESS®
A DIVISION OF THOMAS NELSON
& ZONDERVAN

WestBow Press books may be ordered through booksellers or by contacting:

WestBow Press
A Division of Thomas Nelson & Zondervan
1663 Liberty Drive
Bloomington, IN 47403
www.westbowpress.com
844-714-3454

Some quotations of scripture are only partial quotations of the verse or verses cited.

Unless otherwise indicated, scripture quotations are
from the King James Version of the Bible.

Scripture quotation identified as being from "NIV" is from *The
New Testament, New International Version*, New York International
Bible Society, New York, N.Y., copyright 1978.

Scripture quotation identified as being from "The Amplified
Bible" is from *The Amplified Bible*, copyright 1965 by Zondervan
Publishing House; twenty-fourth printing, 1982.

ISBN: 978-1-6642-1182-7 (sc)
ISBN: 978-1-6642-1223-7 (e)

Library of Congress Control Number: 2020922331

Print information available on the last page.

WestBow Press rev. date: 3/4/2021

For God so loved the world, that he
gave his only begotten Son,
that whosoever believeth in him should not
perish, but have everlasting life.—John 3:16

Introduction

To a world in a hurry, God offers John 3:16:

- One verse that mirrors some 30,000 verses

- Twenty-five words that summarize nearly 800,000 words

- Seven phrases that encapsulate 66 books

The verse is so short, you can tweet it. Jesus spoke the words; in maybe five seconds, one man pinpointed the message of a book—the Bible—that some forty authors wrote over a period of roughly fifteen hundred years. In any time, in any society, in any language, that's 24-karat communication. Gold!

But the best thing about John 3:16 isn't its brevity or efficiency; the best thing about the verse is its substance, its message. This remarkable collection of words gets my vote for the grandest statement ever uttered on planet earth. The statement can change hearts. The verse can change minds. The words can change lives.

In this brief book, I break down the statement by its seven phrases, each packed with meaning, each building on what lies before it, each essential to the complete message of the sentence. Together, as a whole, they beam the glorious light of the gospel of Christ.

Years ago, I saw that light. I saw the light and I chose not to perish but to have everlasting life. I chose heaven, not hell. I pray you do the same.

For God

John 3:16 starts with God; salvation starts with God.

That is, the matter of getting into right relationship with God, the matter of entering the pathway that leads to eternity in heaven, starts with God. Not with you. Not with me. With God.

Christianity is not the story of man pursuing God, trying to win God's favor. Christianity is the story of God pursuing man, trying to give God's favor. In the garden of Eden, after Adam and Eve sinned, we don't see Adam and Eve walking through the garden asking "God, where are you?" Rather, Adam heard God asking him, "Where are you?" God took the initiative.

God is still pursuing lost souls today. Jesus invaded our world. He invaded our world in order "to seek and to save that which was lost" (Luke 19:10). Jesus is the good shepherd who leaves behind ninety-nine sheep in order to find one sheep.

God knows where you are. "If I say, Surely the darkness shall cover me; even the night shall be light about me. Yea, the darkness hideth not from thee; but the night shineth as the day: the darkness and the light are both alike to thee" (Psalm 139:11–12). God can shine his spotlight into your darkest corner. The fact you're reading this book may show he's found you already! He may be shining the light right now. Don't hide from him. Welcome him.

Sometimes Christians testify that such-and-such number of years ago, they found the Lord. Well, I acknowledge there's an element of truth to that. Twenty-seven times the King James Version of the Bible uses the phrase "seek the Lord." "Seek the LORD, and his strength: seek his face evermore," says Psalm 105:4. "The young lions do lack, and suffer hunger: but they that seek the LORD shall not want any good thing," Psalm 34:10 tells us. So, there's an element of truth in a Christian saying he found the Lord. The greater truth, though, is this: the Lord found him. If that person sought the Lord, where did the desire to seek the Lord originate? It came from God. Jesus says, "No man can come to me, except the Father which hath sent me draw him" (John 6:44).

John 3:16 begins with God. Salvation begins with God. One way or another, he reaches out to you and beckons you to himself.

As you read this book, you may feel God tugging at your heartstrings. If you do, don't resist him. As he calls you to come to him, don't dig your heels into the sand. Open your arms and invite Jesus in! If he's tugging at your heart, know that he's tugging with love.

So Loved the World

Mankind didn't take long to mess up. Adam and Eve had heaven on earth, but sinned. Paradise was lost. Society, such as it was, toppled into a downward spiral:

- Cain killed Abel, meaning the first murder we know of on planet earth was committed by the first person we know to be born on planet earth. It also means the first person we know to be murdered was the second person we know to be born.

- Only six chapters into the first book of the Bible, "God saw that the wickedness of man was great in the earth, and that every imagination of the thoughts of his heart was only evil continually" (Genesis 6:5).

- Before Moses reached the bottom of the mountain, the Israelites were breaking one of the ten commandments God had just carved into stone—they were breaking the very first one: "Thou shalt have no other gods before me."

What a sad picture of the human race. The Bible says the human heart is desperately wicked (Jeremiah 17:9).

And yet God loves us.

Every one of us has failed. "For all have sinned, and come short of the glory of God" (Romans 3:23). Yet God loves us. God does not know a sin he does not hate, but God does not know a sinner he does not love.[1] God's love is unconditional. We may tend to love those who love us; God loves everyone. On the cross, Jesus asked forgiveness for the very men crucifying him.

Love isn't just something God has; love is something he is. The book of I John says God *is* love (I John 4:8 and 4:16). Love is at the core of his being. How badly have you messed up your life? Regardless, God loves you. He wants you. Jesus died for you.

God's love is so great it challenges the capabilities of human language. How can we put it into words? Paul prayed the Ephesians would know the breadth, the length, the depth, and the height of Christ's love (Ephesians 3:18). The apostle names four dimensions here where, in fact, only three dimensions of this sort exist. If we were describing a box, we might tell how wide it is from left to right, how tall it is from bottom to top, and how deep it is from front to back. As far as size goes, those are the only measurements we can make. Well, Paul was an intelligent man; I think he knew the three dimensions. Why did he name four? Might he have been writing between the lines? Might he have been saying the love of God goes to the limit of our human ability to describe it and then continues beyond that?

The hymn writer Frederick M. Lehman tried to capture the greatness of God's love this way:

> Could we with ink the ocean fill
> And were the skies of parchment made
> Were every stalk on earth a quill
> And every man a scribe by trade
> To write the love of God above
> Would drain the ocean dry
> Nor could the scroll contain the whole
> Though stretched from sky to sky[2]

Christians often refer to "the peace that passes understanding." There's a love that passes understanding too: "And to know the love of Christ, which passeth knowledge" (Ephesians 3:19).

Years ago I heard a prominent gospel singer say the song inmates requested the most when he ministered in prisons was "Jesus Loves Me." This singer had put some big hits onto the record charts, but the song the prisoners apparently most wanted to hear was the simple children's song that tells of Jesus's love:

> Jesus loves me; this I know
> For the Bible tells me so
> Little ones to him belong
> They are weak but he is strong
>
> Yes, Jesus loves me
> Yes, Jesus loves me
> Yes, Jesus loves me
> The Bible tells me so[3]

You may feel so down in the dumps you wonder whether anyone loves you. Well, the evidence is in. The verdict is clear. God loves you. He loves *you*. And he loves you so much he did something about it.

That He Gave His Only Begotten Son

Here comes controversy.

Controversy in John 3:16?

Yes, controversy in John 3:16.

When God sent someone to earth to pay the price for man's sin and make salvation possible for all, he didn't send Muhammad; he didn't send Buddha; he didn't send Confucius; he didn't send Krishna. He sent his only begotten Son. He sent Jesus.

Jesus isn't *a* savior; he's *the* savior. He's the only one. To believe anything else is to disbelieve Jesus. In John 14:6, Jesus says "I am the way, the truth, and the life: no man cometh unto the Father, but by me."

The message of Jesus's unique position as savior reverberates through the New Testament. Paul wrote it: "For there is one

God, and one mediator between God and men, the man Christ Jesus" (I Timothy 2:5). Peter preached it: "Neither is there salvation in any other" (Acts 4:12).

Does the claim that Jesus is the only way to heaven make you uncomfortable?

Uncomfortable or not, an honest student of the scripture can't immediately dismiss the Bible's statements that Jesus is the savior who excludes any other savior. The statements demand a verdict in the heart of everyone who hears them. The Bible, including Jesus specifically, says Jesus is the only way to God. If we can't believe the Bible on this point, on what point can we believe it? If we can't believe Jesus on this point, on what point can we believe him? In claiming to be the only way to heaven, Jesus either is lying or mistaken or right. If he is lying or mistaken, I don't see how he's qualified to be any savior at all.

The idea that only one way exists to heaven isn't radical. Two plus two equals four. Not three, not five, not any other of the gazillion numbers that exist. I'm not narrow-minded or mean for rejecting all other numbers as the answer to the question. I don't hate eight. I'm not a five-o-phobe. Rather, I am correct. Two plus two isn't a matter of my disposition; it's a matter of truth, of reality.

What is the reality concerning Jesus?

I believe the record presented in the Bible, a book that foretold a rebirth of the nation of Israel centuries before a rebirth happened in 1948. From the record in the Bible, I believe this: No one else lives as Jesus lived; no one else dies as Jesus died. Jesus came to die. Everyone dies, yes, but death was Jesus's purpose. It was his purpose from the moment he was born. No one else can say that. Isaiah 53 foretold a man who would be a man of sorrows; a man despised, rejected, and acquainted with grief; a man oppressed, stricken, and afflicted. This man would be wounded and bruised for other people's sins. He would be taken as a lamb to the slaughter. He would be "cut off out of the land of the living" and put into a grave. Acts 8:26–39 confirms Isaiah was speaking of Jesus.

The concept of sacrificial death was well known in Old Testament times. In obedience to God's word, Israelites sacrificed cattle, sheep, goats, birds. The people killed those animals. They did it to be in right relationship with God. All of those sacrifices pointed forward to an ultimate sacrifice. Leviticus 4:32–35 talks of a person being forgiven by killing a lamb and offering it as a sacrifice to God. Many years later, when John the Baptist saw Jesus, John the Baptist said "Behold the Lamb of God, which taketh away the sin of the world" (John 1:29). Jesus was the ultimate sacrifice. He is the ultimate sacrifice. He, and he alone.

The coming of Jesus was promised by God (as early as Genesis 3:15), prophesied by prophets, and foreshadowed by Old Testament sacrifices. The ancient picture God drew of the coming savior was fulfilled in human flesh by the man born of a virgin in Bethlehem. Jesus is the one whom God sent to save fallen humanity. He's the one and he's the only one.

Jesus is the savior. And that's good news, not bad. Imagine a man swimming in the ocean, just off the shore. Suddenly cramps grab the muscles of his midsection and he begins to sink. In terror he yells to the beach for help. A lifeguard rushes into the water, takes hold of the man, and drags him to the shore. The man survives. What do you think is his reaction? Hundreds of people are on the beach. Do you think he is mad because so many didn't help him or ecstatic because one did?

Suppose a team of scientists finds a cure for cancer. Suppose they are the only ones to do so. Suppose they market their drug and people's bodies are healed and their lives are spared. Will anyone complain because there's only one cure for cancer?

As a former sinner who was headed for hell, I'm not offended there's only one savior; I'm thrilled there's any savior!

In the agonizing hours before he was crucified, Jesus prayed in Gethsemane that if any other way existed to make man's salvation possible, then let that other way be done. After he prayed that prayer, Jesus was arrested, forsaken, whipped, spat on, crowned with thorns, hit in the head, mocked, hung on a cross, and put to a torturous death. Worst of all, he was separated from his heavenly father. "My God, my God, why hast thou forsaken me?" Jesus cried. For us today to say another way of salvation exists is to show terrible and dangerous disregard for the torture Jesus endured and the death Jesus died after he prayed his prayer in Gethsemane. If another way existed, why did Jesus go through all of that? There was no other way. There is no other way. Jesus is the way.

Jesus, God's only begotten Son, is the savior. *The* savior. And he's offering forgiveness and eternal life to you.

That Whosoever

A pastor has just finished preaching a gospel sermon. Moved by the message, a man steps out of his seat, walks forward, and kneels at the altar. The pastor joins the man and realizes he is one of the toughest-looking characters he ever has seen. The man hits the pastor with a blunt question.

"Do you really believe God can forgive anything I've ever done?"

"Yes, of course; the Bible says so."

The man reaches inside his jacket, pulls out a pistol, and lays it on the altar. Next he reaches into his pocket and pulls out bullets. "I'm an enforcer for the mob," he says. "I've used this gun in ways that I don't even want to talk about. Can God forgive me?"

Soon the man and pastor are praying and the man cries out to God to forgive him.

"I still have those bullets on a shelf near where I prepare my messages," the pastor, Dan Betzer, later told in an interview. "When I meet people and it looks like an impossible situation, I look at those bullets and remember the gunman who came to our altar in response to God's incredible grace."[4]

One of my favorite words in the Bible is "whosoever." It occurs in the King James Version 163 times. One time is in the midst of the one verse in the Bible that summarizes the message of the other thirty thousand. John 3:16: "For God so loved the world, that he gave his only begotten Son, that whosoever believeth in him should not perish, but have everlasting life."

Ten of my other "whosoever" favorites from the word of God (bold print added by me):

- "**Whosoever** drinketh of the water that I shall give him shall never thirst" (John 4:14)

- "**Whosoever** liveth and believeth in me shall never die" (John 11:26)

- "I am come a light into the world, that **whosoever** believeth on me should not abide in darkness" (John 12:46)

- "**Whosoever** shall call on the name of the Lord shall be saved" (Acts 2:21)

- "To him give all the prophets witness, that through his name **whosoever** believeth in him shall receive remission of sins" (Acts 10:43)

- "For the scripture saith, **Whosoever** believeth on him shall not be ashamed" (Romans 10:11)

- "For **whosoever** shall call upon the name of the Lord shall be saved" (Romans 10:13)

- "**Whosoever** shall confess that Jesus is the Son of God, God dwelleth in him, and he in God" (I John 4:15)

- "**Whosoever** believeth that Jesus is the Christ is born of God" (I John 5:1)

- "**Whosoever** will, let him take the water of life freely" (Revelation 22:17)

The gunman at the altar was a "whosoever." The thief crucified beside of Jesus was too. "Whosoever" includes the self-described chief of sinners, the Apostle Paul. "Whosoever" includes a former slave trader named John Newton who wrote a hymn called "Amazing Grace." Another hymn writer, Fanny Crosby, got the picture. She wrote, "The vilest offender who truly believes, that moment from Jesus a pardon receives."[5]

You are a "whosoever." You may be a criminal whosoever who never has seen the inside of a church building or you may be a choir-member whosoever who never has admitted your sin or acknowledged your need of a savior. In either case or in any case in between, you are a whosoever. So, the message of the Bible belongs to you. John 3:16 belongs to you. Because of the truth of that verse, the gunman's situation wasn't impossible and yours isn't either. You're not too bad to be saved. You're not too late to be saved. You're right on time to receive the free gift of salvation Jesus purchased for you.

God is a whosoever God. Christianity is a whosoever religion. It's not white-man's religion; it's not black-man's religion. It's not rich-man's religion; it's not poor-man's religion. It's not American religion; it's not Russian religion. It's whosoever religion! The Bible tells us the inhabitants of heaven will come from "all nations, and kindreds, and people, and tongues" (Revelation 7:9).

Today we can see that prophecy being fulfilled. In 2011, a study published by Pew Research Center said persons who identified themselves as Christians made up a majority of the populations of about two-thirds of the world's countries and territories. Don't miss that: folks who called themselves Christians didn't have just a presence in roughly two-thirds of the countries and territories; they had a majority. Among those two-thirds were countries as diverse as Ethiopia, the United States, Russia, and the Philippines.[6]

I realize anyone can say he is a Christian, whether he is or isn't. But regardless of what percentage of these people were true believers—saved, born-again Christians—the fact they identified as Christians speaks to the power of God and to the reach and influence of the gospel message.

The government of China may not tend to pat Christians on the back, but Pew estimated the nation was home to 67 million Christians—a number roughly equal to the population, Christian and otherwise, of California and Texas combined. Along the same line, the Council on Foreign Relations said some estimates showed China on track to have the world's largest population of Christians by 2030.[7]

God doesn't want to exclude anyone. Christianity is for the uppermost to the gutter-most. It's for young and for old. It's for male and female. It's for educated and uneducated. It's for *you*!

Believeth in Him

What determines whether you go to heaven?

If someone posed that question to people on the street, I think most would say God bases his verdict on whether you are good enough. One person would say it one way and another person another, but the common thread would be the belief that you must earn your way into heaven.

I'll go a step further. I believe that if someone were to conduct a survey asking American *church attenders* the requirement to go to heaven, a substantial percentage—maybe even a majority—also would say you have to work your way in.

Wrong!

We can't earn heaven:

- **"By the works of the law shall no flesh be justified"** (Galatians 2:16)

- "God imputeth righteousness **without works**" (Romans 4:6)

- "Who hath saved us, and called us with an holy calling, **not according to our works**" (II Timothy 1:9)

- "But **to him that worketh not**, but believeth on him that justifieth the ungodly, his faith is counted for righteousness" (Romans 4:5)

- "**Not by works** of righteousness which we have done, but according to his mercy he saved us" (Titus 3:5)

(I added bold print for emphasis.)

Our best isn't good enough. "All our righteousnesses are as filthy rags," the prophet Isaiah says in Isaiah 64:6.

All have sinned (Romans 3:23). We do wrong things. We fail to do right things. We're guilty of sins of commission. We're guilty of sins of omission. Even when we do the right thing, we may do it for the wrong reason. In a scenario where perfection is the demand, we, on our own, are hopeless.

Perfection is the demand? Yes. When Adam sinned, God banished him from the Garden of Eden (Genesis 3). God banished Adam not when he sinned twice or three times or four, but when he sinned once. Moses hit the rock instead of speaking to it—we might think that a minor infraction if an infraction at all—and God forbade him to enter the Promised Land (Numbers 20:7–12). James 2:10 says if we keep all of God's law except for one part, we're guilty of breaking it all.

God is holy. He won't tolerate sin. And the result of sin is death (Romans 6:23). Ultimately, this death is separation from God.

God saw our plight and he devised a plan. He formulated a solution.

The solution is Jesus.

God sent Jesus to the earth to pay the penalty for your sins and mine. Though sinless, Jesus was executed as a criminal, dying a torturous death by crucifixion. But God raised him from the dead, and Jesus is alive forevermore. We are saved—we receive our ticket to heaven—by believing what Jesus did for us and accepting the free gift of salvation his death and resurrection make available to us.

> That if thou shalt confess with thy mouth the Lord Jesus, and shalt believe in thine heart that God hath raised him from the dead, thou shalt be saved. For with the heart man believeth unto righteousness; and with the mouth confession is made unto salvation.
>
> Romans 10:9–10

> For whosoever shall call upon the name of the Lord shall be saved.
>
> Romans 10:13

I acknowledge some Bible verses seem to indicate salvation is based on our works. But we have to interpret those verses in the light of the entire Bible. If we could be saved by our works, why did Jesus come?

One day someone asked Jesus point-blank about the matter of works. "Then said they unto him, What shall we do, that we might work the works of God? Jesus answered and said unto them, This is the work of God, that ye believe on him whom he hath sent" (John 6:28–29). The Amplified Bible says, "They then said, What are we to do that we may [habitually] be working the works of God?—What are we to do to carry out what God requires? Jesus replied, This is the work (service) that God asks of you, that you believe in the One Whom He has sent—that you cleave to, trust, rely on and have faith in His Messenger."

Jesus said their work was to believe, to believe in him. As I interpret this, I think we would be justified in putting the word "work" into quotation marks. That is, Jesus is talking about a "work" that really isn't a work. It's a *so-called* work. It's a work *in a manner of speaking.*

The question to Jesus was, what should we do? His answer was, believe.

"Therefore being justified by faith, we have peace with God through our Lord Jesus Christ," says Romans 5:1. Justified by faith. Not by works.

My brain pictures salvation this way: The saved person is lying face down and flat on the ground, motionless and helpless, not even wiggling a finger to try to save himself. He's totally relying on Jesus. I believe that picture lines up with Jesus's story of the Pharisee and the publican (tax collector).

Two men went up into the temple to pray;
the one a Pharisee, and the other a publican.

The Pharisee stood and prayed thus with
himself, God, I thank thee, that I am not
as other men are, extortioners, unjust,
adulterers, or even as this publican.

I fast twice in the week, I give tithes of all
that I possess.

And the publican, standing afar off, would
not lift up so much as his eyes unto heaven,
but smote upon his breast, saying, God be
merciful to me a sinner.

I tell you, this man went down to his house
justified rather than the other: for every one
that exalteth himself shall be abased; and he
that humbleth himself shall be exalted.

Luke 18:10–14

The Pharisee was trusting in his works—the good things he
did do, the bad things he didn't do. The tax collector said
nothing of his own doings; he stood empty before God and
pleaded for mercy. The tax collector was totally relying on
God. He went home saved. The Pharisee didn't.

By human standards, the Pharisee may have been a good man.
But good people don't go to heaven; *saved* people go to heaven.
That is, we don't qualify for heaven by being good. We qualify

for heaven by trusting in Jesus, by relying on Jesus. We are saved by faith.

Why do we struggle with simply receiving God's free gift of salvation? Well, I think our natural human inclination is to try to fix things on our own. When men are lost on the highway, why don't they ask for directions? One, we don't want to admit we're lost. Two, we want to figure things out for ourselves. In many respects, the desire to solve our problems on our own is a good thing, in my opinion. But it's not a good thing in relation to the salvation of our souls. We *can't* save ourselves.

Ephesians 2:8–9 sums up salvation this way: "For by grace are ye saved through faith; and that not of yourselves: it is the gift of God: Not of works, lest any man should boast." It is by grace, through faith. By grace, through faith; this point can't be overemphasized. Grace is God's unmerited favor. Faith is belief. This is the way we become saved. This is the way we stay saved. By grace, through faith.

"Just as I am, without one plea, but that thy blood was shed for me," an old hymn says.[8] The only case I can make for myself is Jesus died for me and I'm trusting in him. Another hymn makes the same point with these words: "Nothing in my hand I bring; simply to thy cross I cling."[9]

Either Jesus or you will pay the penalty for your sin. Jesus already has paid it, but if you don't accept that payment, you will pay the penalty. You will pay the penalty in hell.

The jailer in Acts 16 asked the most important question ever: "Sirs, what must I do to be saved?" The answer from Paul and Silas: "Believe on the Lord Jesus Christ, and thou shalt be saved."

For God so loved the world, that he gave his only begotten Son, that whosoever *believeth in him* . . . . Believeth what? What must I believe? That Jesus, the sinless Son of God, went to the cross and was crucified, paying the penalty for my sin. That Jesus rose from the dead. That if I call on him to save me, trusting in his death in my place, Jesus will save me and I will go to heaven.

Should Not Perish

A man and his wife came home from church one Sunday and the man vowed never to go again. He was offended. He was miffed. The preacher had preached on hell, and this man in the congregation wasn't going to risk exposing himself to such an experience again.

The man's wife was sad to hear her husband's angry words. She kept going to church, but her husband didn't. Weeks went by. Months went by. Years went by, and the man didn't go. Finally, one Sunday, to his wife's surprise, the man rolled out of bed, dressed, and announced he was going to church. The wife was thrilled.

When the preacher—not the same one as before—started preaching, the wife cringed. The preacher was preaching on hell! What were the odds? Why did this happen? The husband had stayed out of church for years after hearing a message on hell. He finally goes back and he hears a message on hell again.

As the preacher concluded, he invited those who didn't know Jesus to come to the altar and be saved. He invited them to escape the horror of hell.

The husband stepped out of the pew, walked to the altar, knelt, and asked Jesus to save him.

The wife was shocked.

At home afterwards, she told her husband she didn't understand. "You stayed away from church for years because of a message on hell. Today you went back, the preacher preached on hell, and you got saved."

"The preacher today," the husband explained, "preached with love and compassion. That other preacher who preached on hell sounded like he wanted me to go there."

Regardless of the impression Christians sometimes may give, be clear on this point: God doesn't want you to go to hell. John 3:16 says so. For God so loved the world, that he gave his only begotten Son, that whosoever believeth in him *should not perish* . . . . John 3:17 continues the thought: "For God sent not his Son into the world to condemn the world; but that the world through him might be saved." II Peter 3:9 says Jesus is "not willing that any should perish, but that all should come to repentance." Jesus came to earth so we wouldn't have to go to hell.

In the scriptures above that refer to perishing, the Bible isn't talking about dying the type of death that newspapers report in obituaries. The Bible here is talking about the "second death." That is, it is talking about going to hell. We see this in

Revelation 20:14: "And death and hell were cast into the lake of fire. This is the second death."

Hell isn't a popular subject and understandably so. It's repulsive. It's repulsive but it's real. Do I want the doctor to tell me I have cancer? If I have cancer, yes. Why? Because then I can do something about it. If you're headed to hell, you can do something about that.

The Bible is clear that hell exists and that people go there. What are the characteristics of hell?

One, hell is a place of torment. Four times in the six verses from Luke 16:23 through Luke 16:28, Jesus, speaking about hell, refers to torment.

Two, hell is a place of fire. A man in hell in Luke 16 wants someone from outside of hell to come and "dip the tip of his finger in water, and cool my tongue; for I am tormented in this flame." Also, Jesus spoke of "hell fire." And Revelation 20:14–15 says hell ultimately will be cast into a "lake of fire" and that "whosoever was not found written in the book of life was cast into the lake of fire."

Hell is horrible. Hell is no joke. Hell is a reality. People who reject Jesus as their savior are going there.

What's the state of a person in hell? I'm struck by the fact the man in hell in Luke 16 seems to still possess his mental faculties. He engages in conversation. He remembers he has brothers still alive on earth. He is aware of his fiery surroundings and he reasons water might comfort him. He seems to have the mental ability to recognize his misery, and we see him crying out for mercy.

One other point—an obvious but important one: the man in hell in Luke 16 is alive and awake; he wasn't annihilated upon his arrival in hell.

Recently I heard a preacher say someone accused him of trying to scare people into heaven. He said his response was, I wish I could! Let me say as respectfully and politely as I can, if you're headed for hell you have every reason to be scared; you have every reason to be absolutely terrified—you *should* be absolutely terrified.

My immediate reason for becoming a Christian was to escape the horrors of hell. I was only a kid, but I had two Sunday school teachers who taught about hell and I was smart enough to know I surely didn't want to go there. So I asked God to save me.

Will you do the same?

The message of hell is harsh, but the good news of John 3:16 is we don't have to go!

But Have Everlasting Life

God doesn't want us to go to hell, but that's only half the story. He wants us to go to heaven. For God so loved the world, that he gave his only begotten Son, that whosoever believeth in him should not perish, *but have everlasting life.*

This everlasting life is everlasting life with him, in heaven. Jesus died to give us that opportunity.

In my book "When Hope Is Lost," I make these points about heaven:

> Imagine the architectural splendor of heaven, or, maybe more accurately, of the city called New Jerusalem. It's described in Revelation 21. The city, we are told, is pure gold, similar in appearance to clear glass. The wall of the city is jasper, underlaid by a twelve-tiered foundation built of twelve precious stones.

The gates of the city are made of pearl and the street of the city is pure gold. What a sight. And yet, as grand as its beauty is, heaven is much more than a pretty place.

Heaven is a place of undiluted blessing. Earth is tarnished by sin. Romans 8:20–22 says creation is in "bondage to decay" (NIV), groaning in pain, yet promised a day of deliverance. Something else is tarnished. This may sound nearly blasphemous, but in this life even God's blessings are tainted.

"Whoso findeth a wife findeth a good thing," the Bible says. Yet this blessing that generates unfathomable joy at the altar produces unspeakable pain at the grave. Such is our lot in this life. In this world, Satan sometimes gets the last laugh, in a sense, over even the blessing given to us by God. Not so in heaven.

Heaven is a place of absolute joy. This is unending joy. This is joy that need not cringe over pain that may replace it, because pain won't be found there. Heaven is a place of no more pain and no more parting. It's a place of no more crying and no more dying. God will wipe every tear from the believer's eyes, and sorrow will be no more.

Heaven is a place of life without fear. On earth, even in good times, we're often glancing over our shoulder to see whether trouble is sneaking up on us. From the time we're babies, crawling on the floor in diapers, fear is drilled into us. "Don't put that in your mouth; you'll get choked." "Don't climb up there; you'll fall and break your neck." The warnings follow us to the grave. Fear permeates our lives. Oddly enough, our desire for what is good sometimes is motivated by our fear of what is bad, and our pursuit of success often is fueled by our fear of failure. Though some danger signs along life's highway are necessary, I suspect they sour our thinking and suppress our freedom more than we realize. In heaven, we'll live liberated from the dread that the ax is ready to fall.

Heaven is a place of life without limitation. Imagine the justifiable sense of invincibility that believers will feel in heaven. Unless our departure from earth occurs when Jesus returns to catch away his people (I Thessalonians 4:13–18), we will arrive in heaven immediately after surviving the most powerful punch evil can throw: death. The worst will be past and we'll be free to live as never before, more alive than a kid on Christmas morning.

Heaven is a place of no stress and no struggle. "No pain, no gain" is the rule of our current existence, a life in which we give in order to get and sacrifice in order to succeed. On earth, every step of progress requires a price to pay. It's a world of trade-offs. Want a higher-paying job? You can have it, possibly, but it may come with longer hours and a heavier workload. By the sweat of our brow we earn our way, in this life. In heaven, contentment comes at no cost.

Heaven is home. At some level, in some way, everyone wants to go home. The student in the classroom and the worker in the mill keep a close eye on the clock, waiting all day for the final bell or whistle to send them home. The white-haired lady in the nursing home, her mind maybe too diminished to remember her name, knows enough to know she wants to go back to the house where she loved her husband and raised her children. On that cold, snowy night when death hurtles the believer toward the unfamiliar landscape of eternity, heaven is the warm, glowing house that will welcome him in.

Finally, and best of all, heaven is a place where inhabitants will experience the endless thrill of an endless existence in the presence of God the Father and Jesus his Son.[10]

In this wonderful place, Jesus offers you an eternal home. Will you accept his offer today?

Conclusion

Your situation couldn't be more black and white.

As you read these words today, you're reading them either as a person who is headed toward heaven or as a person who is headed toward hell. At this very instant, your name either is written in the book of life or isn't. You are saved or you are lost.

We all deserve hell. We've all sinned and fallen short of God's standard (Romans 3:23). And the wages of sin is death (Romans 6:23). This means eternal separation from God.

But God so loved the world, that he gave his only begotten Son, that whosoever believeth in him should not perish, but have everlasting life. John 3:16 happened! John 3:16 happened and now "the gift of God is eternal life through Jesus Christ our Lord" (Romans 6:23).

The question is, do you believe and will you receive? Do you believe John 3:16 and will you receive God's gift of salvation?

If you're headed in the wrong direction, you can turn and go the right way. God is ready, willing, and able to write your name in the book of life.

Romans 10:13 says "For whosoever shall call upon the name of the Lord shall be saved."

Revelation 3:20 gives a beautiful picture of the way salvation happens. Jesus says "Behold, I stand at the door, and knock: if any man hear my voice, and open the door, I will come in to him, and will sup with him, and he with me."

Will you open the door and let Jesus in?

Will you ask him to save you?

Notes and Citations

1   I heard preacher Rex Humbard make this point about God's hatred for sin and love for the sinner. I think I heard it in a program on TV. Later, on the web at https://www.mcall.com/news/mc-xpm-1985-05-20-2470955-story.html, I found the point attributed to Rex Humbard.

2   From the hymn "The Love of God."

3   From "Jesus Loves Me," generally credited to Anna Bartlett Warner, though some sources say William Batchelder Bradbury wrote the chorus.

4   Rick Knoth, interviewer, "The Preaching Life: An Interview with Dan Betzer, Saturnino Gonzalez, and Bryan Jarrett," *Enrichment* (Winter 2013): 49. Published by The General Council of the Assemblies of God.

5   From the hymn "To God Be the Glory."

6   "Global Christianity—A Report on the Size and Distribution of the World's Christian Population," Pew Research Center, https://www.pewforum.org/2011/12/19/global-christianity-exec/.

7   Eleanor Albert, "Christianity in China," Council on Foreign Relations, https://www.cfr.org/backgrounder/

christianity-china. I didn't see a publication date for this article, but as of June 14, 2020, the article was stating it was last updated October 11, 2018.

8   From the hymn "Just As I Am," written by Charlotte Elliott.

9   From the hymn "Rock of Ages," written by Augustus Toplady.

10   Ron Lewis, *When Hope Is Lost: How To Survive When Life's Storms Threaten To Drown Your Dreams* (Xulon Press, 2007), 125–127 . . . . Clarification: On page 31, I mean death (physical death) is the most powerful punch evil can throw *to a Christian*.

Also from Ron Lewis:

Even Christians can lose hope.

The best of believers can descend into despair. Elijah did. David did. Paul did. People familiar with God's power can come to doubt God's provision.

You may be there today. If you are, you don't have to remain in misery. The God who created everything from nothing can deposit hope into your heart again!

You can help him do it. This 182-page book tells how. *When Hope Is Lost* identifies dangers to dodge and principles to pursue.

You can buy the book from its publisher, Xulon Press, or from major online booksellers.